HERITAGE TRACTION IN COLOUR

Volume Two
THE PEAKS

NOSTALGIA ROAD PUBLICATIONS

The **Heritage Traction** Series™

is produced under licence by

Nostalgia Road Publications Ltd.
Units 5-8, Chancel Place, Shap Road Industrial Estate,
Kendal, Cumbria, LA9 6NZ
Tel.+44(0)1539 738832 - Fax: +44(0)1539 730075

designed and published by
Trans-Pennine Publishing Ltd.
PO Box 10, Appleby-in-Westmorland, Cumbria, CA16 6FA
Tel.+44(0)17683 51053 Fax.+44(0)017683 53558
e-mail:admin@transpenninepublishing.co.uk

and printed by
Kent Valley Colour Printers Ltd.
Kendal, Cumbria +44(0)1539 741344

© Text: Trans-Pennine Publishing Ltd. 2004
© Photographs: Author's collection or as credited

Front Cover: *Showing off its steam heating capabilities, 45069 (D121) is filmed at Toton on 21st March 1979. As a class 45/0 it was not fitted with electric train heating and was withdrawn in July 1986, being cut up a year later at Berry's yard in Leicester.* Aldo Delicata (D1000).

Rear Cover Top: *Powering along in typical Peak style is 88 (45136) on a cross-country express near Honeybourne in 1969. At this time it was allocated to the D16 Nottingham Division as were many of its classmates.* John Fernyhough (D1001).

Rear Cover Bottom: *By 28th June 1987 Peaks were often requested as the motive power on enthusiasts' specials. This is demonstrated by 45128 (D113) on a Bakers Dozen Railtour. Arriving at Westbury for the second time, it performs for the cameras and the assembled crowds who appreciated the final days of the class.* Alister Betts (D1002).

Title Page: *In charge of a Liverpool train at Marsden on 14th August 1983, is 45128. A little over six more years of service was ahead of this 45/1, which had originally been D113.* Nick Gledhill (D1003)

This Page: *A trio of Peaks 45106 (D106), 45107 (D43) and 45115 (D81) show off the distinctive style of their noses to advantage at Derby in May 1988.* Steve Ireland Collection (D1004)

INTRODUCTION

As a consequence of the 1955 British Railways Modernisation Plan, the change from steam locomotives to more modern forms of traction was seen as a fundamental part of re-building the railways from the devastated state they were in at the end of World War II.

First steps had been taken towards main line diesel locomotives in the latter years of the Big Four companies. The first of these was based upon the designs of the LMS/BR-built Co-Co's 10000 and 10001 under the guidance of H. A. Ivatt in 1947-8. The second was the trio of designs under the supervision of the Southern Railway's O.V.S. Bulleid, who completed his 1Co-Co1 engines with 10201-10203 between 1950 and 1954.

The experiences with these five diesels played a major part in the decision to build ten 'pilot' engines (which became the Class 44s). These ten were ultimately extended to become the 193 engines of the Classes 44, 45 and 46, which are better known collectively as the Peaks.

Above: *The first of the Class 44s was D1* Scafell Pike, *seen here at Toton Shed a few months after being re-numbered to 44001 in February 1974. A relatively short working life was in store for the first of the class as it was to be withdrawn from service on 30th October 1976, with the remains being cut up very slowly in 1977 at the Derby Works!* Strathwood Library Collection (D1005)

Unlike the five prototypes, all of which had English Electric engines, the ten locomotives in the 'Pilot' order, which would be built in BR workshops were specified with Sulzer engines. As a matter of interest the engines fitted to the other two main line prototypes 10100 and 10800 were of the Paxman type.

At that point in time there was a political mandate that ensured the British Railways Board placed its orders with a variety of manufacturers. As a consequence, another Type 4 (of 1Co-Co1 arrangement) was therefore under consideration from English Electric and it would ultimately become the Class 40s.

It was the lessons learned from the running of the prototypes on the West Coast Main Line (WCML) that ultimately influenced the London Midland Region's order for ten 2,300hp engines. Ironically, it was not for the WCML, but the Midland Division that the Peaks were required, although it was fitting that they were to be constructed at the Derby Works. Interestingly, in a reversal of roles, when the Peaks had been allocated to the southern part of the Midland Division, the English Electric-built locomotives would find much of their early work on the WCML.

As the Modernisation Plan took a view that engines should, as far as possible, be of 'mixed traffic capability' the designs of the new diesels had to reflect this. In turn, this impacted on the overall weight of the Peaks, as this was needed to aid braking in the days of un-braked and loose-coupled goods trains and (at best) vacuum brake-fitted short-wheelbase wagons. Weighing 138-tons, the design was no lightweight and came in at three-tons more than the heaviest of the prototypes (10201 and 10202).

This undoubtedly led to concerns about their Route Availability from the Chief Civil Engineer, which was given as RA7. The Ivatt 'Twins' 10000 and 10001 were RA8 with their Co-Co wheel arrangement, whilst Mr Bulleid's trio were rated RA6.

Work on the 'Pilot' engines was swift, and in the early spring of 1959 the first of the class D1, quickly arrived on the scene. In fact it had taken just nine months from when construction started. The class name Peak would of course be taken from those first ten engines, which were all called after famous mountain peaks. Consequently D1 was named *Scafell Pike* after the highest peak in England at 3,208 feet,

Befitting its important role in the modernisation programme, D1 was put on public display at St. Pancras on 21st April 1959. Thereafter it would spend the majority of its first summer as a test locomotive. Meanwhile D2 *Helvellyn* and D3 *Skiddaw* were named on 11th May 1959 and joined D1 on test until being officially allocated to Camden (1B), although notionally on loan to Derby (17A) until the spring of 1960. D2 was the trial engine up-rated to 2,500hp to meet the new power requirements that were to be ordered for the engines of Classes 45 and 46. This was achieved with an increase to the inter-cooling, but D2 reverted to 2,300hp after the trials in 1959.

Below: *On 22nd February 1977 44002 (D2)* Helvellyn *is seen resting at Toton, where many of the class were based for nearly 20-years.* Steve Ireland Collection (D184)

Interestingly, English Electric delivered D200 their first 1Co-Co1 on 14th March 1958, a full year before Derby Works, as we will see in *Heritage Traction in Colour Volume Four, The Class 40s*. Yet progress with the Peaks was not slow, and by 14th December 1959 the last of the ten had been built. It was named *Tryfan* after the 3,010ft peak in Wales, which overlooks the River Llugwy in Snowdonia.

This not only completed the initial order, but it also saw the last use of a peak or mountain name until the arrival of Class 60s and the naming of several Class 37s many years later. The following 183 engines that would become Classes 45 and 46 followed more traditional naming themes or were left un-named altogether, but what a pity that further Peaks were not named after the Scottish Munros (mountains above 3,000 feet)!

Above: *At Trent Junction in the summer of 1973, we see the recently refurbished 3* Skiddaw, *on a long rake of 16-ton steel coal wagons. Named after the fourth highest peak in England (3,053 feet in the Lake District), it seems that* Skiddaw *was the first to lose its nameplates in July 1976 as it was also the first to be withdrawn and swiftly cut up at Derby Works.* Brian Ireland/Steve Ireland Collection(D1006)

It is said that the operating department wanted engines of 2,500hp instead of the original 2,300hp of the first ten locomotives. This was no doubt influenced by those shed foremen who could see the differences in performance between a Royal Scot 4-6-0 (say with a rake of ten coaches on the St. Pancras to Manchester route) and that of one of the smaller 4-6-0s.

To meet the needs of the operating department and thus avoid reverting back to the old Midland Railway policy of small engines and short trains, the management acquiesced. Therefore it was arranged that the next orders were placed for 2,500hp locomotives, of which Derby Works would build 39 engines (D11 to D49), while Crewe Works was given the job of producing 88 locomotives (D50 to D137).

Both works set about the construction together, so observers would have seen a steady stream of new engines coming out from October 1960 until July 1963. By this time the Eastern Region had expressed a need for allocations of this class to help them replace their steam fleet. Readers are reminded that this is well covered in two volumes from our accompanying British Railways in Colour series, *Steam For Sale* and *From Steam To The Scrapyard*.

The first 15 locomotives (D1 to D15) were all built with gangway doors, so that the locomotive crews could move from one engine to another when working in multiples. One has to recall that these were the days when engines had second-men on board and when steam heat boilers had to be watched. However it was quickly discovered that these gangway doors were both a nuisance and unworkable on several counts.

Below: *The first Class 44 to be painted in blue, seems to have been D4* Great Gable *in 1967, and it may have even retained half-yellow warning panels for a while. By 1970 the overall blue was beginning to look tired as it passed by Derby. Withdrawn in November 1980, ultimately preservation would save the engine and return it to green livery. Incidentally, the peak Great Gable is located in the Lake District National Park and is 2,949 feet high.* Steve Carter Collection (D1007).

Firstly the overall length of all the Peaks was 67 feet 11 inches, certainly far longer than the five prototypes but still a foot shorter than the Class 40s. This meant that on certain tight radius curves, the gangway canvas and its supports would be torn apart. Secondly the practice of actually using the gangways was more of a management and union requirement, with each side having their own motives for so doing. Yet, the practicalities of using them at speeds of up to 90mph were many-fold, not to mention the howling draught that would be inflicted on the crew in the cab as a result of the wind penetrating around the door seals at the front of the nose.

During 1959, and before experience of the traction motors fitted in the first locomotives could be fully ascertained, an order for a further 76 Peaks was placed with Derby Works. This time it specified the use of traction motors from nearby Brush of Loughborough, rather than those from Crompton Parkinson.

Above: *Several Class 44s were to run in traffic in the late 1960s and early 1970s in green, without the body stripe after local repaints at Toton. When the photographer found D5* Cross Fell *at Derby shed in the usual weekend line up in 1966 the old steam age coaling stage was still intact. Just for the record,* Cross Fell *(in Cumbria) is the highest point in the Pennines at 2,930 feet high.*
Steve Ireland Collection (D1008).

In the end the locomotive order was cut back to 56 engines and the final 20 sets of traction motors went into the Brush Type 4s (later Class 47s) instead. By this time the writing was on the wall for Peak production as rather than place orders to extend what was to become the Class 46 fleet, the British Railways Board went for the Brush Type 4 design as the 'standard' diesel class. This saw a further 510 locomotives being produced to this design, and these will be covered in more detail in volumes 5 and 6.

What follows in this book is a visual record of a versatile and well-loved class of locomotive, but I cannot begin without acknowledging my sincere thanks to Alister Betts, Steve Ireland and Colin Whitbread for their invaluable help and assistance!

I hope that you will enjoy this selection of images from the Strathwood Library and that you will be moved to make contact with us, not only to add duplicate slides to enhance your own collection, but also to possibly share with others, access to your own work for the enjoyment of readers in future publications with us. We are always pleased to hear from you in this respect and would welcome requests for subjects for future volumes in the Heritage Traction series.

Kevin Derrick   Scotland. October 2004

Left: *In compiling this volume, we found that 44006 (D6)* Whernside *appears to have been the most camera shy of all of the first ten Peaks. Fortunately our photographer caught it on a Midland line freight at Stenson on Christmas Eve in 1975, instead of being carried away with last minute shopping! The locomotive was to be taken out of traffic in January 1977 and broken to provide spares the following month at Derby Works.* Whernside *is the highest peak in Yorkshire at 2,414 feet.* Adrian Healey/Steve Ireland Collection (D1009)

Top Right: *Your author's first sighting of a class 44 was D7 (44007) when seen from the train at Spalding in the 1960s. It was named* Ingleborough *after one of Yorkshire's 'Three Peaks' (the others being Whernside and Pen-y-Ghent) and is located in Ribblesdale. It also has a distinctively-shaped profile with a flat top and can be seen from the Settle & Carlisle line. When pictured at Toton on 20th October 1979, the engine had only a year of its life left. Furthermore, by this time many of the survivors were showing some pretty ramshackle repairs around the grilles on the locomotive sides.* Aldo Delicata (D1010)

Bottom Right: *Preservation was a saviour for 44008 (D8)* Penyghent, *as by the time of Toton's Open Day in 1979 its future was almost secured. Pen-y-Ghent, which is near Horton-in-Ribblesdale, stands at 2,277 feet and is thus the smallest of the Three Peaks.* Aldo Delicata (D1011)

Left: *For some strange reason it was decided that both D9 and D10 would carry a different style of grille pattern on their sides, which was not repeated on any other class members. Unfortunately for D9 (44009) Snowdon, it was to be involved in an incident and was to receive a 'conventional' nose to one end only. With a wonderful mix of coal wagons in tow, providing a delight and an inspiration for railway modellers, we see 44009 in Toton Yard on 27th April 1978 just eleven months from withdrawal.*
John Harrup (D1012)

Above: *The last of the pilot engines D10* Tryfan *was named on 14th December 1959. Seen in 'economy green' as applied at Toton, it has acquired two differing patterns of window surround in this view at Derby Works in December 1972. We can particularly see that it needs attention to the paintwork, especially where paint has been deliberately removed around the hinges of the nose doors. Ultimately withdrawn due to fire damage near Mansfield Junction on 11th May 1977, 44010 would find its way back to Derby for cutting by July 1978.*
 Steve Ireland Collection (D1013)

The Regiments

Top Left: *Having run through some of the most attractive Peak names in England and Wales already, the Publicity Department of the London Midland Region went back to the drawing board for names. It did not go too far for inspiration, as it fell upon some of the names of the former LMS Royal Scots and Patriot 4-6-0s that the new diesels were then replacing on many duties. As witnessed by 45039 (D49)* The Manchester Regiment, *a name originally carried by Royal Scot 4-6-0 46148. The Peak however carried the name from a ceremony at Manchester Piccadilly station on 9th October 1965 until withdrawn in December 1980. We find it at Taunton in 1976 after re-numbering in April 1975.* John Sansom (D1014)

Bottom Left: *Originally numbered D50 in May 1962 and named three years later in May 1965 as* The King's Shropshire Light Infantry, *a new regimental name to British Railways. When seen at Bescot in 1981 it was to carry the regiment's name only in theory, as the plates on this side at least, have vanished. The telltale bolt holes can be seen on its flanks, it is a pity that the original name was not painted back on in the style of the unofficial namings. Another four years were spent as 45040, before becoming 97412 at withdrawal. It ended its days at M.C. Metals in November 1991, after three years out in the open.* Strathwood Library Collection (D1015)

Top Right: *D52 was named* The Lancashire Fusilier *when just over a year old in a ceremony at Manchester Piccadilly station on 31st October 1963. Re-numbered as 45123 in April 1974 it was always allocated to the Midland Region. Here we find the engine backing on to a rake of MkI coaching stock ahead of a departure from Derby in 1976. Perhaps it was ironic that after so many years of passing through Leicester, this Peak would eventually join the infamous pile of diesel engines at Vic Berry's scrapyard in that city after its withdrawal in July 1986. Records suggest it lost its nameplates in April 1986, whether it ran much in this condition during the last three months we could not tell. However, by July two years later (1988), Berry's had finished the job and its story was over.*
Steve Ireland Collection (D1016)

Bottom Right: *The original naming of D53 as* The Royal Tank Regiment *took place in a ceremony at Derby Works on 24th September 1964, when already two years into traffic. It later became 45041 and is seen here at Severn Tunnel Junction in 1980, where some contraction of the doomed yards at this famous location is already evident. The nameplates were officially removed from 45041 around July 1985, but as we see here (at least on one side of the locomotive) the regimental crest has been removed, either officially or by a souvenir hunter. Fortunately the engine itself was an early survivor in the diesel preservation movement.*
Arthur Wilson (D1017)

Top Left: *Running towards the twilight of its days, we find 45023 (D54)* The Royal Pioneer Corps. *It is being overhauled at Swindon Works (of all places) on 12th August 1980 rather than the Derby Works. This refit was to last it until withdrawal in September 1984 and the subsequent breaking up at Vic Berry's in October 1986. Named in a ceremony at St. Pancras station on 14th November 1963 this Peak went on to set a world record. Loaned to Willington Power Station in the Trent Valley for September and October 1968, it ran non stop for 341 hours (two weeks) during part of its stay there as a temporary generator. In the tradition of its regimental namesake, this engine was a real ground-breaker!*
Dennis Feltham (D1071)

Bottom Left: *A regular in my spotting days at St. Pancras was D55* Royal Signals, *which became 45144 after December 1974. Once again named within Derby Works, this time on 30th June 1965, it carried these nameplates for 21-years but ran its last year in service nameless until December 1987. One of a number of the class to be scrapped at the often over-crowded premises of Vic Berry's yard in Leicester, it had gone by July 1988. The divided centre headcode as carried by many of the class is seen to advantage in this view at Toton on April Fools' Day in 1972. The ever present representatives of Class 44 can be seen to the right, along with what was no doubt one of many Class 20s present on that day to the left.*
Frank Hornby (D1018)

Below: *Another favourite 45137 (D56) The Bedfordshire And Hertfordshire Regiment (TA), is caught on camera at the London terminus in 1978. The naming ceremony for this engine was appropriately carried out at Bedford station on 8th December 1962, after just a couple of weeks in traffic. It had been re-numbered in September 1974 into the TOPS scheme, with all of the ETH-fitted locos being numbered into the 451xx series as a sub-class of 45/1. These modifications began with D96 in December 1972 with the last of them being completed in July 1975 when D78 became 45150. Named after the London parish in which it is situated, the Midland Railway opened its St. Pancras terminus (now sadly a shadow of its former self) in 1868, and for nearly a century it was renowned for having the world's largest station roof without internal supports. The frontage with its grand gothic style was a testimony to both the design and confidence of the new railway age in the mid-Victorian era. At the time of writing, the station along with the adjoining Kings Cross area is under considerable change as part of the new Channel Tunnel station modifications. Our readers will perhaps prefer to remember both of these stations in the days before even the arrival of the overhead wires, which so severely restricted photographic opportunities!*

Jack Hodgkinson (D1019)

Above: *Seen here at Derby Works on 31st January 1979 in the guise of 45043, this engine was originally D58. After just over a year in service it was spruced up for its naming ceremony at Carlisle Citadel station on 1st May 1963, when it became* The Kings Own Royal Border Regiment. *As this engine only had a steam heating boiler, it was numbered 45043 under TOPS. When new, the approximate cost for these locomotives was coming out at around £110,000 each, whereas Type 1s and Type 2s were quoted as costing approximately £70,000 each. While Deltics on the other hand with their twin engines were costing nearly £200,000 each but that forms another story in Volume 3. Around 1978 the management appears to have considered four options to improve the reliability of the Peaks and thus prolong their service lives; these options were as follows: -.*

1   *Rehabilitate those considered for upgrade as Class 45/1 locomotives at their next overhaul, regardless of overhaul classification.*

2   *Relegate all Class 45s to easier workings and replace them with Class 47/4 locomotives.*

3   *Consider their replacement with Class 50s once the HSTs had entered service on the Western Region and Class 50s became spare.*

4   *Finally continue as before and use other classes to share in their workloads.*

Steve Ireland Collection (D1020)

Below: *In contrast to the painted nameplates on other locos, the replacements for 45104 (D59)* The Royal Warwickshire Fusiliers *were made of wood. As seen here at Leicester in September 1987, the replicas were made to a three-line style rather than the original two-line type fitted in May 1964. They were crafted, carefully painted and fitted after the originals went missing sometime in 1986. Along with the modified 45143 seen on pages 19 and 58 this was the only three-line nameplate fitted to the class. As can be seen, further embellishments were painted on by depot staff and the engine enjoyed a brief celebrity status, although as seen here it was not always kept clean prior to its withdrawal in April 1988. Somebody has even painted the clips for the front nose grilles white in their attempt to tidy up this old favourite with a lick of paint. By the time this picture was taken in 1987 the traditional station architecture at places like Leicester Midland was giving way to the more economic building styles of the 1980s. Some may suggest that modernisation was urgently needed, as the old stations were certainly run-down after years of neglect, but even so, much of the railway's character has been eroded during the last 20- years of the 20th century.* Phil Nunn (D1059)

Top Left: *Early re-paints into the full corporate Inter City blue carried the D prefix, as steam was still very much alive on many of the lines they worked around Leeds, Manchester and the Settle & Carlisle line. Even across in Newcastle the dying embers lasted until September 1967. Whilst we do not have an exact date for this view we believe it is at Derby in 1967. As D60 (later became 45022 and then re-numbered again in departmental use as 97409), it carried the name of* Lytham St. Annes *from 1st May 1964 until July 1987. This name was previously carried by Patriot class 4-6-0 45548. Sadly both engines were to be scrapped with 97409 going to M.C. Metals premises in Glasgow by October 1991. The choice of name was to commemorate the forming of the 1st Battalion of The Loyal North Lancashire Regiment, who were formed in the town and went on to fight bravely in World War I.*
Len Smith (D1022)

Bottom Left: *There is not much difference in the standard of finish given by Derby Works to 45112 (D61)* Royal Army Ordnance Corps *when seen 'ex-works' in the yard in January 1974. It had just been re-numbered and refurbished with new electric train heating equipment to work with more modern coaching stock. The High Speed Trains were not far away and British Rail wanted to improve their rolling stock capability on the Midland main line as well as on the cross-country routes for which the class were dominant for 20 years.*
Michael Beeton (D173)

Below: *Making an unusual appearance on the 13.10 Waterloo to Exeter St. David's, 45143 (D62) 5th Royal Inniskilling Dragoon Guards 1685-1985 passes Wimbledon Durnsford Road depot on Tuesday 11th June 1985. This working is in connection with the dedication of the additional nameplate, bestowed to commemorate three hundred years of the regiment. The locomotive was taken off the service at Andover. Unfortunately 45143 was only to carry these plates for less than two years as it was withdrawn in May 1987. However it did linger around before eventually moving to M.C. Metals in Glasgow to become one of the last Peaks to be cut up in March 1994.*
Colin Whitbread (D1023)

Left: *Bringing out the empty stock from the sidings at Paignton in June 1974, 63* Royal Inniskilling Fusilier *gets ready to take holiday-makers back to the Midlands and the North. The illustrious name was previously carried by a Royal Scot class 4-6-0 46120, and the Peak taking over the name at Derby Works in September 1965. The records show 63 as shuffling back and forth between Cricklewood and Toton several times that summer, as rosters were changed with the arrivals of ETH fitted 45/1s. However 63 was to become 45044, as it was not sanctioned for ETH fitting in March of 1975. This was yet another named Peak to go to Glasgow for breaking up, and it suffered the ignominy of running the last few months nameless in service.*
Arthur Wilson (D1024)

Above: *Another name taken from a Royal Scot 4-6-0 (this time from 46114) was* Coldstream Guardsman. *Taking over the honour of the name was D64 on 24th April 1965 three years into traffic. By February 1975 it had become 45045 and it is in this guise we catch the locomotive heading a coal train south out of Toton yard on Wednesday 25th August 1982. A class 31 can be glimpsed in the distance and at this time the yard was still very busy with coal trains before the effects of the miners strike. So the observer would be rewarded with frequent train movements throughout the day and with engines coming on and off the shed as well.* Coldstream Guardsman *was to be withdrawn by the next summer with final cutting at Vic Berry's yard by October 1987.*
Ian Beckey (D1025)

Top Left: *Staying with a Guardsman naming theme D65 was named as* **Grenadier Guardsman** *on 23rd May 1964, two years after leaving Derby Works as a new engine. Several of the Peaks hung on to their green livery with half-yellow fronts for some time, even though the class was being re-painted rapidly into blue at the works and at depots from as early as 1966. This shot on 18th February 1968 found the engine proudly carrying the name that once adorned Royal Scot 4-6-0 46110. The twin warning flashes in this view are in what were the standard positions for them on centre headcode-fitted locomotives. Later in August 1973, it would be released to traffic with electric train heat as 45111 for another 17-years useful duty.* Frank Hornby (D1026)

Bottom Left: *Many of the regimental names seem to have been fitted at Derby Works without ceremony! One of these was fitted to D67* The Royal Artilleryman *in September 1965, using a name that was previously carried by a Royal Scot 4-6-0 46157. It is a pity that today's locomotives do not celebrate some of our famous regiments, and the valuable service they have given both in the past and present; perhaps another tradition of the railway being allowed to slip by. Our view shows the name fitted when the locomotive was re-numbered to 45118 on the diverted 07.50 Newcastle to Liverpool at Garswood on 28th March 1982 some three years before withdrawal from service and a further life in preservation.* Leonard Ball (D1027)

Below: *The Derby to Birmingham main line was a happy stomping ground for spotters looking for Peak action, and a visit to the lineside at Wigginton near Tamworth on 22nd March 1967 rewards us with D68 (45046)* Royal Fusilier. *Once again a Royal Scot, this time 46111 was the original bearer of the name; the Peak having only been carrying this name for nine weeks, since the 21st of January 1967. Clearly in the short time since the name was fitted, the paintwork would not have gone downhill this fast, so the clean red nameplates and crests must have been fitted to a pretty shabby engine in Derby Works without much ceremony. Or was this soldier perhaps wearing camouflage? Modellers should also note the interesting long wheelbase van behind the engine at* this time. *The breakdown of the headcode 7M91 is interpreted using the* British Rail Headcodes ABC *from Ian Allan for that year. The figure 7 denotes the class of train, in this case an express freight not fitted with a continuous brake. While the second character (M) denotes the destination region of the train as the London Midland Region. The third and fourth characters 91 suggest that this train is bound for the Nottingham Division and Spondon or Derby. But one assumes that the signalmen along the route knew of the train and its destination, both by the working timetables and the box to box communications as they tried to fit its running between the path of express passenger workings.*
Paul Barber (D1028)

Top Left: *This picture shows where the combined handholds and steps once gave access to the steam heating boiler water filler hatch on 45048 (D70)* The Royal Marines. *It is seen on 29th August 1981 whilst on the 09.35 Liverpool to Paignton as it stands by Platform 1 at Exeter St. David's. Having been named at St. Pancras on 2nd December 1964, the engine was built with split headcodes. These split headcodes were a legacy of the idea to have connecting doors. Even though the doors were not fitted, the already fabricated headcode boxes were still used!* Ian Beckey (D1029)

Bottom Left: *Wearing the 'economy blue' livery first applied to at least 11 of the class from 1966, is D71* The Staffordshire Regiment (The Prince of Wales's). *Another late name application at Derby Works this time on 20th May 1966, perhaps this was the time that the blue livery was applied? It seems that after checking through many hundreds of shots of the class that these early blue repaints did not carry either the new or the old style of logo. As can be seen from this view and a further shot of one of the early repaints (on page 49), the shades of blue were different to the official Rail Blue adopted by the British Railways works. Named after the combined North and South Staffordshire Regiments. This old soldier ended its days as 45049 in April 1989 in Glasgow, at the hands of M.C. Metals as did so many of the Class 45s. Our view is of happier times at Bristol Temple Meads in 1968.*
Steve Ireland Collection (D1030)

Above: *Still wearing the original split headcodes is Crewe-built 45004* Royal Irish Fusilier, *which dates from 1960. As it thunders along with a loaded rake of 16-tonners at Harpendon back on 14th June 1975, it is typical of what was then a daily sight on the Midland main line. From the headcode 8C15, we can surmise that this is a through freight train not fitted with automatic brake, and was destined for the London Division. However, the ABC lets us down, as it does not suggest where 15 was a destination, but perhaps not surprisingly since the last of these handy little books was published in February 1968! Whilst this was still known as D77, it was called to Derby Works in September 1965 to receive a name from a former Royal Scot locomotive (46123). This was another locomotive to run its last year nameless as the plates seem to have been removed in October 1984.*
Aldo Delicata (D1031)

Below: *Stabled in the yard at Nottingham over one weekend during 1978 our picture shows 45055* Royal Corps of Transport, *a name it acquired at Derby Works on 18th June 1966. Keen-eyed readers will clearly observe that, with a ridged edge, it carries a rather different style of nameplate from the majority of class members.*

Entering traffic on the very last day of 1960 with a working life of 25 years, the engine was to join the famous pile of engines including classes 03, 08, 20, 25, 26, 27, 31, 33, 37, 40, 47, 76, 82, 83, 84 and 85 who have all lost class members within Vic Berry's scrapyard in Leicester while it was open for business. Arthur Wilson (D1032)

Above: *Royal Scot 46144 was origina lly named as the* Honourable Artillery Company, *but D89 acquired the name during 1965 at Derby Works. Re-numbered to 45006 in November 1973, fellow spotters of the day will recall that the pages of their 'combines' tended to look untidy as they scribbled in the amendments to the re-numbering of the Peaks between 1973 and 1975, while the ETH programme was being carried out. This view shows 45006 at Exeter St. David's with the 09.58 Leeds to Paignton on 29th August 1981, which would have been packed with holidaymakers heading to the south-west. The pattern of Peak workings into Devon changed at the end of the 1960s at a time when the Warship Class diesels were being withdrawn. Consequently, the previous engine changes on these inter-regional express workings (which had been at either Bristol or Gloucester) were progressively dispensed with, and the Peaks ran all the way through. In addition to the normal workings at this time, which followed the Midland route from Leeds to Sheffield, duplicates were often run via Dewsbury, Huddersfield and Penistone to cater for the extra passengers and some 'Golden Rail' party bookings. The destination station, Exeter St. David's was originally opened as a broad gauge station by the Bristol & Exeter Railway, later absorbed into the Great Western Railway, becoming dual gauge in the 1870s. The station was then rebuilt just before World War I and has fortunately changed little since this time.* Ian Beckey (D1033)

Below: *Sheffield Midland was always a good place to see Peaks in the 1960s, 1970s and into the 1980s as well. A visit here in February 1977 finds 45059* Royal Engineer *standing light engine in the station. Five and a half years after being built as D98 the name of the former Royal Scot was taken up on 20th December 1966 at Derby. It was to carry this name for 20-years, before finally coming out of traffic in March 1986 and finding its way to Vic Berrys in Leicester for breaking up by July 1988. It seems strange that England's 'Steel City' which had been notorious in the past for the scrap yards that broke up so many of the British Railways steam fleet did not take a very active role in the dismissal of the diesel fleet that followed. One exception to this rule is perhaps Messrs Booth Roe Metals with their yard at Rotherham. But, even so, considering how often Peaks passed by their gates over the years only one 45106 (D106) was to be taken inside for processing in 1992. This perhaps reflects the voracious appetite of Vic Berry's yard during the 1980s. For those readers interested in this more macabre side to our railway history they are directed to* Steam For Sale *and* From Steam To The Scrapyard *in the British Railways in Colour Series* Roger Griffiths (D1034)

Above: *The name of 3ʳᵈ Carabinier was applied to D99 at Derby Works in December 1965, but had previously been carried by 46125 from the Royal Scot Class. The Peak that acquired this name was later re-numbered as 45135, but our picture still finds it in the guise of 99. It is seen running fast with a long rake of General Utility Vans (GUVs) at Trent Junction in the summer of 1973. The split headcodes seem to have been panelled over during 1978 on a visit to Derby Works. A long time resident of first Derby then Toton, it was a regular on the former Midland main lines. The problems and confusion over the re-numbering of the Peaks has already been mentioned, but it is worth noting that even British Railways had problems over it. For example whilst 78 was re-numbered to 45054 in January 1975, 95 was given the same number four months later and the original 45054 became 45150 in July. So from mid-May until mid-July there were two locomotives numbered 45054 on the TOPS computer! It is supposed that the first one (78) was probably in Derby Works for ETH conversion at this time. It was withdrawn in May 1987 and fortunately taken into preservation.* Steve Ireland (D1035)

Left: *Exhaust haze as 45060* Sherwood Forester *accelerates hard away from the stop at Bristol Temple Meads in July 1976. Previously numbered D100 and named in a ceremony at Derby Midland station on 23rd September 1961, four months after entering service at Derby (17A). The regiment's name comes from the Cardwell reforms of 1881, which brought together the 45th and 95th Regiments of Foot with the Militia of Nottinghamshire and Derbyshire plus the volunteer regiments of the two counties, to form The Sherwood Foresters (Derbyshire Regiment). It is of interest that it was not until 1902 that Nottinghamshire was added to the title.*
The regiment also fought in World War I where they won many battle honours and were at El Alamein in World War II. Always a favourite name, this particular engine was a popular choice for preservation when it was eventually withdrawn in December 1985. Carrying the four noughts in the split headcode panels gives a strange goggle-eyed appearance to the engine. Roger Griffiths (D1036)

Below: *Named at Chester station on 12th June 1966, D137 carries the name* The Cheshire Regiment, *previously worn by Royal Scot 46134. As one of the earlier repaints into British Railways Inter City blue, it is seen still carrying the D prefix during 1968 at Manchester Piccadilly station.*

The headcode shows H, which was the code for trains heading south of Manchester and on to Stoke-on-Trent. Although it was the last of the Class 45s to be built, 45014 was cut up by Vic Berry's on a crash site at Ashbury August 1986 after sustaining accident damage. Brian Hopkinson (D1037)

Above: *Just one Class 46 was to bear an official name given by BR, with D163 being named* Leicestershire and Derbyshire Yeomanry *on 14th April 1962, in front of invited guests and the public at Derby Midland station. Re-numbered as 46026 in February 1974, the engine later went into storage in September of 1980. Its enforced 'rest' was thankfully short, as it was restored once again to traffic two months later. However, its November 1980 return at Gateshead was without the nameplates as they had gone missing! New plates were then made and fitted at Gateshead on 27th March 1983 in order to restore some dignity. The final withdrawal came in November 1984 with the engine being broken up at Doncaster Works the following March. It was nicknamed 'The Lady', which was made up from the initials of the name.*

We find it propped on the blocks in the depot yard at Doncaster in 1978, where we can see the substantial construction of the bogie frames, but despite this they were very prone to periodic cracking. As a consequence, it was not uncommon to find the bogies being removed for attention at either a depot or the works. However, this picture also reveals a questionable practice employed at that time, which looks as dangerous as jacking up an automobile on bricks. Of course, work methods at many locomotive sheds in the 1970s were little changed from the days of steam, and quite often it was a case of 'make do and mend'. Needless to say, any work of this nature today would involve the locomotive being supported on a purpose-built set of jacks or lifted by crane.
Arthur Wilson (D1038)

RINGING THE CHANGES

During their careers on our railways the appearances of nearly all the Peaks was to change almost continuously, either by mechanical improvements or changes in work practices and traffic needs. Some changes were due to repairs following accident damage and sometimes simply by the progressive changes of locomotive liveries to suit the mood or fads of the time. These changes have occurred throughout the history of our railways, but for the Peaks their number was impressive. For this reason, we have tried to choose a selection of accurately-dated pictures that reflect the number and variety of changes.

Above: *As mentioned, D11 to D15 were originally built with gangway doors between the headcode boxes as seen by D15 (45018) posing on the turntable at Bristol Bath Road (82A) on 4th September 1966. At this time it was allocated to Holbeck (55A) and would have been a regular visitor to Bristol after working cross-country expresses, especially in the days when the hydraulics worked many of the trains down to the south-west from Bristol. The original fixed type of side nose grille as seen here was to give way to a more practical variety with hinges and clips, thus allowing easier access to the nose for those fitters who were charged with the job of maintaining the traction motor blowers.*
Frank Hornby (D1039)

Above: *Compared with the previous picture, 15 has had a complete makeover in this view at St. Mary's Derby on 29th May 1969. Among the external changes, a careful observer will note that the handrails to the cab doors have been modified as well. When built, D11 to D19 and D68 to D86, all had the longer handrails. Over the years various external modifications took place, including the battery charger sockets being moved from the solebars to a new position on the bodyside behind a new hinged cover. To help prevent frost damage to steam heat boilers, a plate was fitted over the small grille at the No. 2 end and so the list went on. As a makeover*

exercise this was carried out on at least 27 Class 45s from 1967. Interestingly, even after all of this, the former D15 still has the original handholds up to the water filler even though the spread of 25,000 volts catenary was well underway on the West Coast Main Line, and the just as deadly 1,500 volts could be found on the Woodhead route where the class might also be found. It is no wonder then that a shiny new warning plate has been affixed near the top of the steps. The orange warning cantrails and full plating up of these handholds on the Class was to come later on.

Michael Beeton (D183)

Top Right: *Wearing an unusual headcode panel and looking more like a fruit machine with four noughts up is 46022, watched by the spotters at York on 15th July 1977. Built as D159 and entering service at Derby (17A) on 24th March 1962, this locomotive spent most of the 1970s as a Western Region engine, before it went into store at Swindon Works on 5th October 1980. Withdrawn on 14th December 1980, it was kept intact and officially reinstated to Gateshead as from 22nd November 1981, although it did not actually leave Swindon Works until 4th March 1982. The reprieve was short-lived however, as it was withdrawn from Eastern Region operating stock on the 28th of that same month! It went back to Swindon Works again the following December, where it was finally cut up by March 1983.* Brian Ireland/ Steve Ireland Collection (D1040)

Bottom Right: *Dragging a 'dead' 46017 at Bristol Parkway, on 7th March 1978 is 46025. Both engines were allocated to Laira at the time and they met again when they were consigned to store at Swindon Works on 5th October 1980. Both were again withdrawn on 14th December 1980 and once more they managed to get reinstated to Gateshead on 22nd November 1981. They left separately with 46025 finally being cut up at Doncaster, and the other returned to Swindon for one last time. By the time of this picture the twin dot 'domino style' had been widely adopted for headcode panels.*
Roger Griffiths (D1041)

Above: *When it was new, D170 was allocated to Gateshead (52A), going there on 21st June 1962. It was then to spend most of its life in the North East and as such was almost a Gateshead engine born and bred. In fact it only spent one month away, when it was loaned to Haymarket and Dundee for crew training in August 1970. It was withdrawn at Gateshead in May 1981, but was sent to the former GWR works at Swindon on 22nd October 1981. After attention it was sent back to Gateshead on 2nd February 1982, where it lasted in service for another 14 months before being finally withdrawn on 19th June 1983. It then moved first to Tinsley and then Gloucester before arriving back at Swindon on 22nd October 1983, where it was cut up a year later. By the time we see 170 basking in the sun at Gateshead in September 1973, the use of the headcodes was fading, and many engines could*

be seen working with some unfathomable headcodes displayed. At first glance, some may think that the electric overhead warning flashes were superfluous, as the short overhead electrified line to the Quayside branch on the banks of the Tyne had closed. However, there were still the overhead lines at Westoe Colliery in the North East to worry about, along with the overhead catenary at Birmingham New Street, which 170 (46033) might be expected to pass through regularly on cross-country trains to and from Newcastle. In addition to these flashes, the plating over of the steps up the loco sides was a sensible precaution. Both locos seen here look to have a non-reflective finish to the top of the nose, which cannot be grime as the roof of 170 is quite respectable; was this a local modification to avoid the problems of reflected light for the driver?

Below: *Ultimately the presence of the overhead electrification would be seen on the East Coast Main Line during the latter part of the service lives of the Peaks, as witnessed here at Kings Cross. Sharing its time between allocations to Gateshead and Holbeck during its working career, 46055 was built as D192 and it went into traffic along with D191 and D193 on 18th January 1963, thereby completing the orders for the Peaks with all of the last three going to Gateshead (52A). A regular at the London terminus over the years, we find it in charge of the 20.00 Kings Cross to Aberdeen sleeper service on 22nd November 1977. This was to be another of those back and forth stored engines between Swindon and Gateshead, only to return one last time! It was to be broken up by November 1984, seven years after this scene.*

Whilst the effects of the headcode lights and the cab lights look bright in this view, the reality out on the main line was not so good. This was however, a significant improvement over the dim oil lights used on most steam engines. The fitting of electric marker lights to some locomotive headcode boxes had helped, but not significantly. Worse still was the dim red oil-lit tail lamp that each train carried, and which were all prone to fall off from time to time. For years the railway unions argued the case for better illumination, but along with the universal adoption of AWS and Automatic Train Control/Protection, safety requirements seemed a very low priority for the cash-strapped BR management and it would be several years before powerful head or tail lamps came to be in common use. Colin Whitbread (D1043)

Top Left: *This selection of night-time images reflects that scenes such as this were re-enacted night after night for many years, as the railways never slept. For example, 45113 (D80) is waiting at St. Pancras for its train to be filled with newspapers that would be delivered to various points along the Midland main line. This shot taken about 1980 reveals that, although passengers are in short supply, other activities are progressing; note for example the Permanent Way Department's crew-bus parked on the platform, presumably its gang are attending to track inside the station. Meanwhile, as the cab lights on 45113 burn brightly, we might assume that its driver was perhaps taking time to read the new day's papers, hot off the press.* Strathwood Library Collection (D1044)

Bottom Left: *Meanwhile, we can see that when 45142 (D83) was captured on a night time working at Bristol Temple Meads, the surviving Peaks were being fitted with an additional high intensity beam. However, only the ETH-fitted class 45/1s were thus equipped, not the steam heat 45/0s. We might mention as an aside that all of the class 45 and 46 Peaks were built with vacuum brakes only but were later converted to dual braking, leaving the class 44 Peaks as 'vacuum only', and working freight trains or the odd special! Five months after this picture on 10th January 1987, 45142 would take its last trip to Glasgow and M.C. Metals to be finally broken up by March 1994.* Alister Betts (D1045)

Above: *The late 1980s saw a number of specials run for enthusiasts to enjoy Peak haulage and for photographic stops. One such stop was made by 45106 (D106) on 13th February 1988 at Kirkby Stephen on the Settle and Carlisle route, one of their great stomping grounds in earlier years. By now, just twelve months away from being withdrawn, this was one of many that had been unofficially named at Tinsley and Toton, in this case 45106 had become* Vulcan. *This was a popular name for locomotives through the years, with a War Department 2-8-0 90732, Britannia 4-6-2 70024 and of course Class 47 D1676, which (along with the other original named 47s) will be covered in Volume Five in this series. The Peaks were almost in sole charge of the Settle & Carlisle expresses for over 20 years and their loss would bring a further change to the character of the line. This station was called Kirkby Stephen West until 1968, it then closed in 1970 and reopened in 1986 two years prior to this shot. It has subsequently been extensively refurbished, and provided with an over-line footbridge to connect the platforms. This can be a cold and bleak location at 860 feet above sea level and the town of Kirkby Stephen lies a mile and a half away and three hundred feet lower. The town had a much nearer station, Kirkby Stephen East, located at the junction of the NER lines to Barnard Castle, Penrith and Tebay. It too has been granted a new lease of life and is currently part of the scheme for the re-opening of the Eden Valley Railway.* Phil Nunn (D1046)

Above: *Many of the un-named Peaks that survived into the late-1980s were to gain unofficial names, which were enthusiastically painted by the depot staff at both Toton and Tinsley. By 2nd February 1988 the former D42/45034 had been transferred into departmental stock as 97411 and received the name* Topaz. *We find the engine glinting in the sun high up on the moors at Penistone under the gantries for the now closed Woodhead 1500v DC electrified route. These were the last few months in use for this engine working out of Tinsley, as by July of that year it was withdrawn, only to head north to Glasgow and join many of its classmates for dismantling by M.C. Metals.*

This company, who had been weaned on steam locomotive dismantling, managed to claim 54 of the 127-strong Class 45s. Of interest in this atmospheric view are the steel girder gantries that once supported the catenary designed by Sir Nigel Gresley. Had this famous engineer had his way, and not seen his electrification plans scuppered by the intervention of World War II, then much more of the former LNER system would have been electrified to 1500v DC. If this had happened, then the future for dieselisation in this country could have been radically different, and perhaps the Eastern Region Peaks, (based on the designs of the LNER's arch-rivals the LMS) may not have been necessary. Nick Gledhill (D1047)

Top Right: *A real mouthful of a number, ADB968024 started life as D23 on 8th April 1961 as a split headcode locomotive allocated to Derby (17A). Re-numbered to 45017 in May 1974, it went on (as indeed did most of the class) to have their noses re-skinned at Derby. Now Taken into engineer's stock, the spacing of the new number is a little too long to get into the space available. At what is thought to be at the end of the staff safety training wiring at Toton on 26th September 1985 we find the locomotive stabled alone. The codings for the depots and stabling points that survived into the 1970s all took on two letter codes from 6th May 1973, with Toton assuming the prefix TO. In June 1993 this was yet another Peak that would be sent north to M.C. Metals in Glasgow for breaking up.*
Adrian Healey/Steve Ireland Collection (D1048)

Bottom Right: *To reinforce the point that some Peaks actually kept their headcode boxes down to the very end, our photographer captured 45027 at Swindon Works on his visit there on 2nd April 1983. It is looking slightly cross-eyed and its paint has faded from sitting out in the open for so long. It arrived at Swindon by mistake as it was initially booked to go to Derby Works on 20th July 1981 for disposal. By September 1983, the one-time D24 had been cut up by the men of Wiltshire who were to get much more practice in the cutting up of Class 46 Peaks rather than those of Derby Works.*
Steve Ireland Collection (D1049)

Left: *Toton started to embellish Peaks from 1979, with some extra detailing in contrasting colours of grilles, adding side stripes again, as displayed by 45013 at Peak Forest on 27th July 1986. A similar scheme was applied to 45022 except with red buffer beams. It is believed this was the last 45/0 to go through Derby Works. Originally fitted as a split headcode engine when new as D20 on 20th February 1961, it later acquired the unofficial name of* Wyvern *painted on its side. For the record, 45012 (the former D108) became* Wyvern II *in these unofficial namings.* Steve Ireland (D1050)

Top Right: *This next pair of Peaks were to find themselves fatefully associated later on in 1983. Firstly we see 46023 (D160) having arrived at Newcastle Central with the 19.37 from Bristol Temple Meads on 17th November 1981.* Colin Whitbread (D1003).

Bottom Right: *One locomotive that was to get a very radical makeover was 46009, seen here at Kings Cross on 11th December 1981 showing its steam heating capabilities to great advantage on what is obviously a very cold evening. Taken into service as D146 on 16th December 20-years previously, its allocations over the years being to depots on the LMR, WR and ER. Then on 23rd October 1983 it was transferred to the Railway Technical Centre at Derby and allocated the number 97401, which it never took up in the end and when it was sold on to the Central Electricity Generating Board, its fate was sealed.* Colin Whitbread (D1051)

Above: *I am sure all of our readers will remember tuning in to the news and seeing the grisly end that awaited 46009 on 17th July 1984 at the Old Dalby test track. To dispel the public fears of a train crash involving a nuclear flask, the engine was adapted to run with cameras on board and be controlled so as not to require a driver to set it in motion. It was then deliberately crashed into a flask (empty of course) at 100mph as a publicity test for the flask! This is the scene on the day, at the point of impact. The horrific effects of such a crash, were maybe enough to satisfy the public at large over the safety of the nuclear flasks, but your author feels they did little to inspire confidence of the effects of a rail crash in MkI rolling stock! Nor did it demonstrate the safety of locomotive crews in high-speed accidents! Ironically the engine was not booked as withdrawn until 23rd July 1984, presumably the delay was while they found all the bits again, and the remains were cut up on site. The spare engine or potential standby was 46023 originally numbered as D160 . CEGB (D1052)*

Below: *Reminding ourselves of what Class 46 locos looked like when brand new, we find D184 and D185 at Derby in the October sunshine of 1962; behind them D183 can just be seen in the shadow of the Test House. Allocated to Gateshead (52A) on 16th October 1962, D185 went on to become a resident of Holbeck, Bristol (Bath Road) and Cardiff Canton before returning to Gateshead in October 1976. It was re-numbered as 46048 in March 1974 whilst still a regular on those turns allocated to Bath Road. Nevertheless, it was a relatively short-lived Class 46 as it was to catch fire near Gloucester in August 1981. It was thus taken to Swindon Works on 20th November 1981 and cut up there by September 1983.*

Whilst some of the Peaks were released to service in all over green, the addition of the small yellow warning panel certainly improved visibility to those on the trackside. In contrast to the pristine-looking Peaks, closer inspection of the picture reveals that vestiges of steam locomotive disposal is still going on at Derby as several old boilers can be seen. The demise of the steam fleet and its replacement by modern traction brought out some unusual statistics. Take for example, the capacities of the Peaks, which were 190 gallons of lubricating oil, 1,350 gallons of boiler water, 346 gallons of engine cooling water and 840 gallons of diesel fuel when full.
Richard Sinclair Collection (D1053)

Above: *Wearing one of the economy green repaints carried out at Toton (and perhaps other depots as well) in the later 1960s is D25 at Kettlebrook near Tamworth on 6th September 1967. This exercise whilst smartening up the engines between works visits, omitted the light grey stripe along the side of the locomotives, although on many the grey roof panels and grille details were retained. A confusing time really as many engines were then repainted at the depots into blue with half yellow ends and the British Railways emblems painted over during the same period, as per D71 on page 24. Allocated at this time to Holbeck (55A), D25 went on to become 45021 in October 1974, and was broken up at Swindon after being one of the very early casualties of Class 45 to be withdrawn in 1980 in the early class run down.* Paul Barber (D1054)

Below: *It is perhaps inevitable that various interpretations of livery would be found when depot repaints are considered, as seen by the yellow warning panel on D165 on the top of Saunderton bank with a football special for London on 3rd April 1965. Allocated as D16 Nottingham Division at this time it must be assumed to have been the work of Toton. It was not a fortunate engine, for as 46028 it caught fire whilst rescuing a failed HST service on the approaches to Plymouth station on 1st May 1984 after its fuel supply pipe fractured. Once it had cooled down it was taken off to Laira and was then sent to York on 10th May! It went back to its home shed at Gateshead on 15th May, but the Geordies cannot have liked what they saw. It was sent for scrap to Doncaster Works and broken up by January 1986.* Richard Icke (D1055)

Below: *Not all Peaks were subject to early repaints into blue or to lose their stripes as seen by D138 at Toton depot in 1971. It is believed that these full yellow ends were not applied until sometime earlier in 1971, having survived with half yellows until then. Built as the first of the order in what were to become Class 46, it entered traffic on 28th October 1961. Like many of the Peaks, it was kept allocated to Derby (17A) before moving on to other sheds. Re-numbered as 46001 in February 1974 it was to join 37 others to be broken at Swindon Works, as British Rail tried to keep the workforce active until closure of the works. It seems British Rail were not keen on outside contractors breaking up the Class 46s as only 46027 went to Vic Berry at Leicester. Aside from the remains of 46009 cut up on site at Old Dalby, the remaining class members to be cut up were six at Derby Works, whilst Doncaster Works disposed of seven. Although this was the first of the Class 46s, it was withdrawn and scrapped by the time that the last five examples were withdrawn from Gateshead on 25th November 1984; these final survivors were 46011, 46025, 46026, 46035 and 46045* John Fernyhaugh (D1056)

Above: *Variations in colour schemes are seen again on 21st May 1967 at Holbeck (55A), which was a great Peak stronghold for many years. We do not have the number of the engine in blue with full yellow ends and we cannot be sure that it is in the Inter City blue rather than an economy blue repaint (like classmate D119 to the right). Two further green Peaks can be seen. The one on the far right still has connecting doors and is believed to be D14 while another lurks in the shed, no doubt several more Peaks were on shed that day.*

Railway modellers should note the faded and weathered red buffer beams, which were attached to the bogies rather than the locomotive body. Perhaps it was the long wheelbase of the bogies and absorbing the strains of the buffer beams that led to many of the stresses and cracking problems associated with the class. This may have been compounded by their use on colliery spurs or tracks with very tight curves, for which they were simply not designed.

Frank Hornby (SH151)

Above: *Showing that at least some of the earlier Inter City blue repaints carried red buffer beams, D186 is seen here with D175 also at Holbeck (55A) this time on 16th November 1967. Compare this against ex-works engines in the pre-TOPS era on pages 5, 18, 31 and 34. Later re-numbered as 46049 in February 1974, it went on to join the multitude in the long lines at Swindon Works, which many of us will remember as various diesel classes went there for disposal from 1970 up until closure of the Works.*

A Class 47 still in two-tone green accelerates hard away on the high level lines in the background with a train of mixed blue-grey and maroon MkI coaches. The red Gresley coaches behind the two Peaks are part of the breakdown train and like the wonderful water crane in the foreground are lovely period reminders of the 1960s. So few photographers seem to have recorded these scenes for us, but if you were one that did, please get in touch.
Paul Barber (D1057)

50

Below: *Among the Class 44 celebrities at least towards the end of their reign was D4 or 44004* Great Gable, *seen here restored to its green livery at Toton on 24th October 1980. Again carrying the stripe and red buffer beams all subtly weathered in traffic, it reminds us of the 1960s. However, the sharp-eyed will notice that in addition to the TOPS number and the boiler access steps being plated up, it is carrying a larger totem than those originally used. Nonetheless it is always pleasing to see the nostalgia for the past recreated with the addition of painted nameplates. The originals were taken off, it seems about November 1980, when it was sold into preservation. It must have been a quiet day at Toton, as normally the locomotive that you wanted to film would always be boxed in, as is demonstrated by so many other views taken here. A Sunday visit to Toton shed in the 1960s or 1970s would usually produce a huge number of engines for a spotter, but teasingly one could only find either eight or nine of the original ten Peaks. More often than not at least one of their number would either be at the works or out on a Sunday engineering train, thus ensuring most spotters had to go to Toton at least twice, or sometimes three times, to record all of the Class 44s.* Leonard Ball (D1058)

Above: *With the crests above the nameplates still very much intact, we find 56 (45137)* The Bedfordshire and Hertfordshire Regiment (TA) *in command of a mixed fitted goods train near Derby in the summer of 1972. Sadly the overall atmosphere of a run-down and neglected system was very much evident on large parts of British Rail during the latter part of the 1970s, with little pride being shown in stations, rolling stock or locomotives at that time. There was certainly little prestige in named locomotives, especially when many of the plates and badges were crudely removed; including those on 45137. Later on things did improve, and in June 1986 a three-line style of replacement nameplate was fitted to 45104 as it became a well-kept pet of both crews and* enthusiasts alike. By the time of our picture we also see that 56 is carrying an unusual middle windscreen. Perhaps it has been repaired with the aluminium surrounds as a replacement, or could it be that it was just leaking badly with perished rubbers? This style of modification seems to have been carried out haphazardly on many of the views we considered for this volume in the series. By carefully checking photographs that were considered for this book, we can see that changes had been made to the nose ends over the years, including those with the central releif in the headcode panels even before the wholesale plating-over of the headcode boxes.

Steve Ireland Collection (D1021)

Below: *Perhaps real celebrity status was to be displayed by 97403 named as Ixion in 1985 after being taken into departmental stock in December 1984. The ex-46035 and D172 before that, had various modifications as part of its new duties, the most obvious being the cutting back of the lower bodywork panels together with its new smart livery. Developed to provide a test bed for experiments with adhesion it was perhaps a surprise that a 138-tonne loco was chosen? Interestingly, for scholars, the name Ixion is taken from Greek mythology from one who was punished by Zeus and bound to a winged and flaming wheel, perhaps aptly named, thinking of all that potential wheelslip!*

Always a favourite for appearances at open days and exhibitions and later restored back to green in preservation by record producer Pete Waterman, it has been out again on the main line, thus confirming its status as a real star! We see Ixion on display at Bedford Open Day in 1987 back in those days when Stock, Aitken and Waterman records were high in the music charts! It is interesting to think that this soon to be preserved Class 46 was indirectly funded by all those who bought his records! Another Class 46 retained to supply spares to Ixion was 46045 (D182), which was to be re-numbered 97404, but thankfully it also made it into the salvation of preservationists. Jim Bryant (D1060)

Above: *At the end of their lives, several other Peaks attained celebrity status and they emerged in special re-paints, of which the original green was widely appreciated. One of those celebrities 45106 (D106), was sadly to be forgotten about as it slipped quietly into oblivion at Booths of Rotherham in April 1992. Nevertheless, with this picture dating from 20th October 1988 we can remind ourselves of the time when Peaks used to appear regularly at St. Pancras. The clock has been turned* *back as 45106 appears in green once more, although it carries the 'Yorkshire Rose' emblem of Tinsley depot on a plate on each side of the engine and cast Inter City arrows under the driver's window. To provide better illumination, a high intensity warning light is fitted to the front, albeit painted black. D16/45016 and D106/45106 were the only two Peaks in Class 45 to maintain their original numbers after the application of TOPS numbering. Steve Ireland Collection (D1061)*

Below: *We have selected this pleasing angle of 45110 (D73) by Leicester North signal box to demonstrate the orange cantrail lining position and the black anti-glare panel above the nose. However, it should be remembered that this panel was difficult to reach and often filthy as a consequence, and this also served to reduce the glare bouncing back at the drivers. Originally fitted with a split headcode D73 was subsequently converted to electric heating only and air braked, but neither these modifications nor its good-looking condition would not save the engine from a trip to the breakers in Glasgow when withdrawn later in 1988.*

The picture is also evocative as it captures many traditional Midland Railway features, the most imposing of which are the warehouses in the background. The signalling is worthy of note also, as semaphore signals from three eras (Midland Railway, London Midland & Scottish Railway and British Railways) could be found at this time along the former Midland main line. Railway modellers may also consider Leicester North box as a possible conversion of the traditional Midland signal box kit from Airfix. It would however, take three or four such kits to re-create this wonderful structure.
Phil Nunn (D1062)

Above: *A number of non-standard re-paints appeared on the Peaks during their latter years, and here we find 45133 (D40) with its cab roof looking like it has been exposed to the frost. It is found at March depot on 5th April 1990, in company with 45108 (D120). Thankfully, this pair have both since made it into preservation and are just two of the 17 members of the 193-strong class that have survived the scrap men. During the late-1960s and into the 1970s, March depot would have seen* regular visits by Class 44s and Class 45s on coal workings from the East Midlands. Visitors to March at the end of the 1980s and the beginning of the 1990s will perhaps recall the long lines of withdrawn locomotives and rolling stock that were stored unattended in the yards. This included a number of Peaks that were easy prey for the vandals, but at the same time allowed enthusiasts the easy opportunity of photography and exploration. Colin Whitbread (D1063)

Below: *We have shown that several Peaks received a variety of modifications to their noses over the years, but D18/45121 had two sessions of 'cosmetic surgery'. It was built with a split headcode nose, but it was later modified to a single panel headcode in the late 1960s or early 1970s; later still it was plated-over completely and joined most of the class in the style with twin spotlights. It is seen here at Derby on 14th May 1981, after it had received the attentions of Toton's painters sometime during 1979.*

Along with 45110, it had gained two white stripes along each side and red buffer beams. This engine was broken up by Messrs T. Hill at Derby Works in September 1993, and as such was the only Peak demolished by this contractor. In addition to the scruffy condition of 45121, the depressing scene at Derby (so common on BR in the early-1980s) is not helped by the way in which the distinctive concrete platform canopies have weathered badly over the years.
Steve Ireland Collection (D1064)

Top Left: *All of the original Peaks in the D1 to D10 series were fitted with this simple style of nameplate without any badges. This one belonged to 44008* Penyghent *(the smallest of the Three Peaks of Yorkshire). Happily this locomotive can still be seen in preservation, although it is believed the original nameplates went to British Rail's 'Collectors Corner' and were sold seperately to the engine. However on 9th September 1979 they were still fitted when this shot was taken at Toton depot. Of note is that the actual spelling of the mountain is Pen-y-Ghent (from the old British/Celtic language) and not as seen on the nameplates.*
Aldo Delicata (D1065)

Bottom Left: *As we have previously seen on page 19, 45143 (D62)* 5th Royal Inniskilling Dragoon Guards *was given an extra embellishment to mark the 300th anniversary of this particular Dragoon Guards regiment. This took place in a ceremony at Andover station on 11th June 1985 where the additional plates seen here were duly unveiled. Take note of the grey roof-line and all the various little data or descriptions plates fitted along the sides of these engines as various modifications were made over the years. For instance the plate to the left of the nameplate was fitted to cover a ventilation grille close to the steam-heat boiler, which was retrospectively fitted to help prevent frost damage. Also visible is the data panel showing Peaks were only rated to 90mph.*
Alister Betts (D1066)

Top Right: *Displaying the more common style of nameplate fitted to the regimental Peaks is 45144* Royal Signals *seen in June 1985, just a couple of years from withdrawal. Sadly, many of the badges which were attractive brass wrap-overs to the actual nameplate, were often damaged in the latter years by attempts at theft. It appears that many of the Peak nameplates were cast in resin, rather than the traditional materials of brass or aluminium; surely given the overall weight of the locomotives the extra few pounds would not have made that much difference!*
Alister Betts (D1067)

Middle Right: *This edged type of nameplate seems to have been fitted to D53/D77/D84/D98 as well as D99 (45135)* 3RD Caribinier. *The crests on some of the class were chromed as well as being painted with additional detail and looked great sparkling in the sun when polished up as if on parade. As can be seen in these three views, the actual shades of red used on nameplates varied and often faded badly. Some of the class had their plates painted black and the details were picked out in silver paint; as for example* The Royal Tank Regiment, *which ran like this for several years.*
Aldo Delicata (D1068)

Bottom Right: *To accommodate the full names of the regiments, several Peak nameplates were in two-line format as seen on 45137 (D56). It proudly bears the crest of a Territorial Army regiment and this reminds us of the importance of these units both in peacetime as well as times of war.* Alister Betts (D1069)

Above: *As late as 9th February 1989 a long line of Peaks could still be found at Derby, although by then it was a melancholy row containing 45148/45126/45146/45125 and 45111 all withdrawn. Stored out in the open at various points around the network, were the other later survivors awaiting the scrap contractors, now that Swindon had closed and Doncaster was no longer actively cutting up engines. It might have given more chance to the preservation movement if many of them had not been so badly vandalised where they were stored at locations, without a great deal of security. Many of our readers will however have gained the chance of cabbing a Peak during this time and seeing the driver's view along the bonnet nose for one last time.* Phil Nunn (D1070)

We hope that you have enjoyed this look back at the Peaks and will join us again in further volumes. A reminder that all of these published shots are available to purchase as superb duplicate slide copies direct from Strathwood. Send £5.00 for an extensive catalogue listing of these and many thousands of other shots available in fabulous colour, complete with sample slide.

Or visit the websites www.strathwood.com or www.railwayslide.co.uk

*All images copyright original photographers or Strathwood Limited. **No reproduction without prior permission.***